the light between the trees

a collection of poems
on healing

alysia quinn

Rising Lotus Press
a division of Rising Lotus Co., LLC
Lakewood Ranch, FL 34202

For more, visit www.alysiaquinn.com
@alysiaquinnpoetry

ISBN: 979-8-218-10343-9

Library of Congress Control Number: 2022917369

Cover Design by Jayson Quinn

if you find yourself
in the darkest night,

may you
hold on.

love is here
and light is on the way.

for ethan & olivia

darkness and light
grief and joy
falling and rising
unlearning and reclaiming
remembering and becoming
withering and blooming

between these spaces, i flow.

what if your story, as is,
matters more than you realize
right now?

what if you didn't minimize
your pain or compare your story
to anyone else's?

what if the parts of your life,
the ones you never want to think about,
and the ones you revel in,
could collectively change the world in some way
by sharing and connecting
with others?

what might happen?

-invitation

Table of Contents

darkness.

for each of us,
there comes a time.
an awakening.
an invitation.

for healing and self-discovery.

the pull comes gradually
and all at once.
and when it does,
maybe we find ourselves
laying on the cold bathroom floor
or staring into our own eyes
or driving with the windows down.

may we pause to listen
to our bodies and our hearts.
may we be curious
and courageous
when that sacred and holy
part of us says,

ok,
it is time
to go out
into the deep.

dark days and soft sheets,
layers of blankets and thick emotions.
this body,
heavy like the ocean.
this mind,
like raging storm waters,
wrestling with invisible people.

a wordless state
with stagnated inhales
and forceable exhales,
a muck of existence.

trying to make sense
out of things
that will never make sense,
wanting to justify
what cannot be justified,
and exhaustion from trying
to figure it all out.
so I don't have to feel
any of this
anymore.

-the suffering

i feel you creeping
in that bottom space,
between the bedroom door
and the hardwood floor.

oh darkness.

your black smoke
fills my nostrils,
your harrowing sounds
permeate with past pains
and images i would like
to forget.

you've descended
and infiltrated
all the nooks,
all my safe places.

and it looks like
i will have no choice,
but to make space for you
for a while.

the madness erupts.
a frenzy
with an unpredictable nature,
utterly unwelcome,
without boundaries or concern.

when i least expect it,
you steal and consume me
with reckless abandon.
my first inclination
is to raise these fists
and shove you back down
from wherever it is you came.

because it takes so much.

space and breath
and movement
and the care of another's eyes.
to help settle in
and to feel like this body is mine again.

-anxiety

these nights
bleed into the days.

in all the dark hours,
one question pervades
my mind.

why all of this pain?

these days,
everything hurts.
every hair.
every bone.
and this skin crawls
in places
that don't even feel
like my own.

i am slowly being devoured,
bite by bite.

and the only thing left
to do
is scream.

i know,
that you know,
precisely
where to find me.

and i am painfully
aware
you're not coming.

and it will never
make sense
to my heart,
not ever.

this new found space
away from you
feels like both
abandonment
and freedom.

these heavy clouds,
covering my eyes,
are like warm blankets
on cold mornings.

and the sun
that beams
happy light
through this window,
only burns my face.

i don't know
what hurts more.

the fact that
you used me,
never saw me,
and discarded me
when you were through.

or the shame i feel,
about actually missing you,
the good parts of you.

from this room,
the echoes
of little voices
and footsteps
in the stairwell.
dishes clanking
and knocks
on the door.

and life.
my life.

it moves on
without me.

-disappearing act

the loss,
not a single loss,
but overlapping generational
stories
of dysfunction
and destruction.

taking breath from lungs,
and light from eyes,
and demolishing
these bones
down to a powdery dust,
with sweetly scented notes
of love's baby soft.

these feelings
flood this body
with unstoppable force.

what is it
you want with me?

i am listening.

-the aching

maybe first,
it was easier
to feel the anger.
throwing punches at walls,
screaming at invisible faces.

until this voice
became a hoarse whisper.

until the rage ceased
and i found myself
sitting in this darkness.

until the numbness
wore off like old perfume
and all that was left
on this skin
was the salty residue
from sadness
seeping out through every pore.

somewhere trusting,
that the sooner
i felt it all,
the sooner
i could start
to heal.

layers of vibrancy,
one by one,
they let go.

the petals
that fall
from the poppies.

teaching me
to do the same.

to empty,
to lament,
to move through
the process
of falling apart.

until i am
bare-skinned,
a flower
without her petals.

this waking comes,
not in the early morning light,
but in the darkest night.

from inside this room
under covers.

from a distance,
i listen and behold her beauty
as the nightingale sings
from outside my window,
a night song that calms and softens.

a melody, slowly unraveling
all the knots
holding this heart and body together

-the undoing

she felt it coming
from deep within.
the past. the pain. the harm.
it had to begin here.

-the roots

what happens
when the entire script
for your life
changes?

what happens
when the shoreline
is a distant memory
and you feel yourself
slipping
into deep waters?

sometimes,
our only next step
is to
ask
for
help.

dear God,

will you mother me?
will you father me?
will you hold me?
will you help me?

in the silence,
the quiet,
the abyss.

something else
has room
to appear.

call it truth
or divine wisdom.
call it whatever we like.
it is there and it speaks
something of universality,
without lines
or shapes.

ominous settles overhead,
and these black clouds
ground and awaken
my soul.
they remind me
of this grief
i still carry.
heavy. intense. inescapable.

and just before
the thunder rolls
and the rains release,
i wait for that cool
rush of air,
the one that caresses my face.

and i can't help
but think,
that must be my God,
kissing my cheek,
telling me,
"the storm is here,
but so am I."

slowly but surely,
the darkness
began to disappear
from her eyes.

she was left
with an aching heart.

and she would see
that the darkness
was the price
she would pay.

to find her voice
and bring it forth.

unearthing.

only from the depths
of darkness
am i close enough
to dig out
these bones.

a slow and dirty
process
of reclaiming
and rebirthing.

-unearth

she laid in the bottom
of that barrel
for a long time,
longer than she ever
thought she could last,
gasping for breath
and praying for help.

until the spirit
that created the wind,
brushed against
the back of her bare neck,
with kind relief
and sweet rescue.

to show her
that this was part
of the necessary process,
one she was blind to
in the present,
and that her surrender to fall
was the only way
up and out.

you were awakened
by the grip
of pain and loss
and you fought it
like a warrior.

but what you believed
would be a battle
in your mind,
began first
in your body.

a shifting
here and there,
your once breathless space
loosens,
cool drops
fall to your face
and glimmering light
offers warm wonderment.

delicious relief
here
in the dirt.

what is this?

-it is hope

she went along
to get along,
until her defiance
began to make
an appearance.

her mind brimming
with questions
that no one
seemed to be able
to answer for her.

she had to find them
for herself.

-the journey

not every place
offers the necessary space.
sometimes old wounds
can't heal
in the old places.

i had to go
find myself
and i could not
take you with me.

so many years and tears,
trying to live in a wasteland,
with blood patterns inherited
and so much work to even see them.

shame follows me
and my head plays games,
thinking of all the things
i should have done
or said along the way.

and maybe you will see
or understand one day,
how i could not stay.

i had to go
live by the sea,
where peace flows
and the pelicans
fly free.

every wave
that crashes,
washes
you away.
and yet,
the tide
keeps rolling in.
each time,
returning more of me
to myself.

she made the choice
to fight
in a different way.

each day,
brave offerings to herself.
each offering,
a defiant act of love.

to find her fierce,
by first,
finding her soft.

before she could go
any further,
she had to ask herself,
whose voice was guiding?
who was the ghost over her shoulder?

i never felt
like i belonged
anywhere.
except sitting
on the inside
of my own head.
somewhere between
wonder and melancholy.

some of us
are looking for words
to make us feel
seen and heard
and understood.

because the things
we've gone through
made us
hurt and hide.

and we desperately
need tending
from the light.

-so, we must name

don't rush
wherever you are.
place one hand
on your heart
and the other
on your belly.

feel the movement
of your breath
with the rising
and falling
of your chest,
the natural order
of ups and downs.

slow down and settle
into your softness,
your tenderness.

you are learning
and it is ok
to be right here.

when we recognize
we are finally
in a safe place,
we receive
the first key
unlocking the door
to our bodies,
allowing the universe
to guide
through the unknowns,
through the releasing.

and ever so slowly,
with the loosening
of knuckles,
joint by joint,
finger by finger,
we begin to unfold,
from tightened fists
to open palms.

remember how brave you are.

displaced but homeward bound
and guided by constancy,
the north star ushers.

what glorious and agonizing attempts
i make to find ways
to speak the unspeakable.
an ache to name,
a wayfarer of words,
and in the waiting, the listening.
for what the echoes
may whisper back
from the cavernous places
i inhabit.
to fill the anguishing silence,
yet hold it with reverence,
as the compass needle
pulls and shifts my course
by the constellations.

and from the palm of my hand,
i'm taking what feels like,
the long way around.

when you alone cannot see hope
or any possible restoration
for what was lost,
when the pain of truth
cuts too deeply,

give yourself
permission.

to sit with the grief
for as long as you need
and to let someone else see you
and sit with you.

you are not a burden.
sometimes we must borrow
someone else's hope
for a while.

she tried so hard
to live up to the picture
someone else painted
for her life.
she was stuck in a system
based on validation and performance.

until she harnessed
the necessary courage to look within,
blessing her true desires,
and offering her own heart compassion.

until she learned
how to mother herself.

with the conviction
to take that painting
and rip it up
into a million little pieces.
and take back what was hers
in the first place.

-reclaim

out of pure desperation
and lament,
laid an unexpected
antidote for pain.

to seek beauty,
in the midst of chaos.

and from the stirring,
to then create.

allowing acknowledgment
and access to that pain
on a deeper level.

somehow bridging the gap.

which, by the way,
is much narrower
than one would think,
from grief and sorrow
to
truth and goodness.

it took the care of others,
sitting with her,
looking into her eyes,
and holding that sacred space.

to help her name
what needed to be named,
allowing it to come forth.

it took the care of others,
sharing the load
and bearing the pain.

to show her
that love and belonging
would gift her
the necessary courage.

for her heart to re-open
to new possibilities.

only then,
could she see,
what all the grief
was trying to teach her.

even if
you do not find
what you think
you are looking for,
don't give up.

keep walking your own path.

your body
and spirit,
in perfect timing,
will show you the way.

some things
stay hidden
from us
for good reasons,
until we are ready
to see them.

i choose love.

by allowing
all of the words
to fall out
onto this page,
without judgement.

i will no longer
abandon myself.

i long for
the grounding song
she sings,
echoing deep within
the back of my throat,
where strength meets grace
and i hear her being received,
with the invitation,
to feel the vibration,
of her weight and force,
the outpouring
of herself,
with full release and trust,
reminding me it is ok to fall.

-waterfall

so often i try
to reduce myself
into a profound
message in a bottle.

except,
i am made
of thousands
of messages
in bottles.

as i have searched
the oceans over,
looking for
that one thing
that makes me feel
like i am enough,
i see,
i will never be
just one thing,
except curious.

-and enough

all i can promise
is that i will do my best,
to keep removing
these layers
of masks.
that keep me away me.
and me away from you.

only grace
allows me to release you
from these
white knuckles.

and i watch you
slowly drift.

away from me.

up into the billows
of smoke from the fires
you never extinguished.

tell me another way
to save myself,
and i'll listen.

instead of numbing it,
offer the ache
an invitation.

it will inevitably
find a path within you
to pass through.

it may write.
it may sing.
it may paint.
it may build.
it may play.
it may dance.
it may make.
it may move.

it will speak.
it will guide.

the gift
of this sadness,
is that to endure it
requires my
moment by moment
presence.

and in doing so,
i've noticed
how those tiny flowers
grow
in such unexpected places.

it is a quiet pain.

not often understood
or easily conveyed,
but i carry it.

and deep down,
i know
it will never
leave me.
because it is embedded
into the very fibers
of who i am,
that which becomes
both heavier
and lighter
over time.

what matters
is how i learn
to carry it.

every day,
with intention,
she stood up
and shook the dust
off her feet.

each piece of her,
made from the stars
that shine
in the midst
of a dark sky.

she sat
legs crossed
in a patch of buttercups,
dreaming up mystical adventures
and naming the stars.

she thought about
which nearby tree
would make the best house
and how she might build it,
so she could always
be in this place.

and more than anything,
she wanted someone
who was looking for her,
who understood her,
to come find her
and stay for a while.

i am
slow sipping
sorrow
and it is hard to do
from this lakeside bench,
while the dragonflies
dance in delight,
and the blue heron
takes flight,
and the magnolia tree
flowers
begin to unfurl,

like me.

how does
the bird
make its way
south for winter?

how does
the baby turtle
make its way
to the ocean?

they find their way.

and so will you.

by following the light
and that pull
in your chest.

what will it take
to know thyself?
curiosity asked.

and love answered.

my dear,
first there will be
a descent
into the darkness.

then,
you will need
an inordinate amount
of persistence.

and finally,
you will gather
all the courage you can hold
in both hands,
to bring forth whatever
it is you find.

i thought i lost
who i was
a long time ago,
but she was there,
deep down inside,
fighting for me
every step of the way.
she helped me
to survive
with her silence,
now she's teaching me
who i am
with her words.

-the poet

maybe you had to
leave yourself behind
to survive.

maybe the treasures
you hold
are buried
so far down within you
that you aren't sure
what they are
or where to begin
to find them.

i
hope you
keep searching.
keep asking.
keep trying.
keep going.

how far down
must we dig
to recover
ourselves?

until our faces and elbows
are caked
with muddy crust
and we finally reach
whatever must be
unearthed.

rising.

we rise
by settling in
to the earth
beneath us.
it has been there
offering us support
all along.

inhale,
feel the dirt
between your toes.

exhale,
make roots.

in the stillness,
her body
began to whisper.
from the darkness,
she made her
appearance.

i met her
here,

the heroine
within.

dirt beneath nails,
sweat drips across brows,
with grit
in the muck.

tending to the soil
of her spirit.

and it is here,
that weeds are pulled
and seeds are sown.

with the first hopeful signs,
revealing something beautiful
is about to rise up.

no doubt about it,
it is terrifying
and will cost you something.

to let others in.
to sit with you.
to be with you.

in your pain.
in your trauma.
in your grief.

but what if
that is the only way
to set yourself free?

if this next part
has you tightening your jaw
and trying to rid yourself
of the pit in your stomach,
maybe
you are right where
you are supposed to be.

you've felt this before
and you know
the growth and beauty
that comes on the other side
of hard things.

settle in, softly.
and press on.

before she could feel
her own strength,
she felt her own fragility.

her body shook
through all
the uncertainty.

and it was both
the reaching out beyond herself,
and the fighting within herself,
a relentless pursuit
to become.

she became willing
to offer herself
what she needed most,
by walking through
the wilderness within,
compassion in one hand
and grace in the other.

she gifted herself
with enough safety.

the safety necessary
for her younger self
to emerge.
to speak.
to grieve.
to heal.

for so long,
she wanted to live
a life
outside of the boxes.

with baby steps,
she finally saw
that she could choose
to do things
differently.

she could learn
to dance with her shadows
and her light.
she could be brave enough
to own her fears
and desires.

and she could insist
on moving towards
a life she designed,
one full of
creativity.

-self care

she had a choice
every single day.

to choose
a path of destruction
or
a path of beauty.

find out
what breaks
your heart.

a song of love.
a dance of despair.
a photo of injustice.
a poem of grief.
a story of loss.
someone's desolate eyes.

sit with it,
with them,
with yourself,
and ask questions.

watch your feelings
emerge,
and bear witness,
as your beautiful
curiosities
lead you home
to yourself.

in her deep sorrow,
a shift of grace,
to rise and not succumb.

from seemingly nowhere,
a push forward,
moving through
all the mud.

accepting this path
as growth,
a resilient act
she never saw coming.

holding steadfast
to her belief,
that light and goodness
are coming for her.
no matter what today
feels like.

-the lotus

especially, in the difficult times.
she knows beauty is as integral
to her being
as air.
and it welcomes her,
heals her,
and asks her to stay.

she yearns
for the grandeur
of postcard scenes,
the obvious kind.

but she's learning
how beauty resides
in the everyday
and the everything.

and that she can find it
whenever she goes
looking for it.

let the old rules go.
the ones keeping you small
and fenced in.

take fear by the hand
and have coffee together.
thank her for keeping you safe
and then walk her to the front door.
tell her she won't be needed
until next time.

good mothering
to your own heart
involves knowing
when to make space
and knowing
when it is time
to release.

different seasons
bring
different energies.

maybe it's rest,
maybe it's strength,
maybe it's something else,
and wherever we are
is ok.

sometimes we cannot see
the reasons
until the season
has passed anyway.

we might as well settle in
and be here
with this one thing.
it will shift
when we are ready.

a pilgrimage
without certainty,
full of rivers to cross,
sights to behold,
and valleys to bear.

and the only requirement
is to show up, everyday.
no matter what that looks like.

this journey promises nothing
but possibilities.

not all progress
is readily visible.
little by little,
hour by hour,
day by day,
all the work
builds layers.
and then after
how ever long it takes,
usually longer
than you think you can bear,
you finally behold
something new.
don't stop now.

some of us
have root systems
strangling our souls.

and we courageously
prune what needs pruning
in order to save ourselves.

and once we do that,
we can't ever go back
to the way things were.

at least,
not with honest eyes.

because the growth
we have witnessed in ourselves
becomes brutally and beautifully
undeniable.

the tough decisions we make to heal
can be unsettling to others around us.

those close to us and most comfortable
with the old versions of who we have been
may offer us resistance
instead of the support we hope for.

may we have faith to search,
high and low,
far and wide,
for our tribe,
the tribe that is for us
and willing to grow with us.

and may we listen
to that good and guiding force within,
when it asks us to uncomfortably
step out and into the light,
even if it means
we take those first few steps
alone.

you remind me,
it is ok
that sometimes i breathe fire.
inhaling complexity
and exhaling intensity.

and when the night smolders
from what the flames left behind,
you hold my hand,
helping me to settle in
to all of who i am.

and when i can't see the space
in front of my face,
you're here and i know
i'm not alone.

and then the smoke fades
enough for me to see
the light between the trees.

and i become aware
that from all that darkness,
i am clearing a new path.

she calls to me,
somewhere between
before and after,
between
first light and dusk,
here and there.

i feel her,
the before her,
wanting more.

the way she used
to touch her own body,
with delicacy
and tenderness.
thin straps resting
on soft skin
and strong shoulders.

sun, moon, and stars
soaked into her wrists.
she yearns for her own scent,
her innocence,
the way she gave
and loved.

it takes but a few moments
to pause and reflect
on how time has passed
through what feels
like several different lives.

and then i see,
i am and always will be,
in the deepest part of my soul,
a precious and needy child.

i learned
to leave you behind,
over time.

i learned to numb you
and sabotage you
for all of your
so-called imperfections.
it was easier to blame you
and i wasn't ready
to look under this skin.

i thought forgetting you
meant i wouldn't have to feel
anymore of this pain.

but you forget nothing,
you patiently hold it all,
you are my wisest friend,
my truth teller.

-dear body

every curve
of this body,
every soft fleshy inch,
i am learning
to own
as mine
and more than enough.

she wanted
to want to settle,
but she's a runner
with a gypsy soul.

and deep down
she knows home
is everywhere
and nowhere
at all.

it may not look anything
like what i had hoped for
or how the world told me
it should be.

acceptance of the truth
was a heart wrenching process
that nearly took the breath
from these lungs.

and the pain you inflicted
was the biggest game changer
of my life.

but now,
i stand here thankful.
because i would not have
what i have
or be who i am today,
without you,
one of my greatest teachers.

she heard it said before
that you are well on your way to healing
when you don't cry anymore
when telling your story.

but she wasn't sure
she believed that to be true.

because calloused hearts harden and build walls
and some kinds of pain will always be painful,
no matter how much work is done
or how much time passes.

and somehow she knew her heart would always bleed
for the goodness she desires in a world that is fallen.

and the blood that
drips and collects needs space,
and she will spend a lifetime
shedding skins and tears,
while growing in her capacity,
to hold it all
and let it all go.

hold on.
let go.
hold on.
let go.
hold on.
let go.

and a good cry
and a good laugh
felt all the same.

at the end of the day,
sometimes the only closure
we will receive
is the kind we can choose
to offer ourselves.

the deviations and detours,
the ones you fretted
and questioned,

remember how
they unexpectedly
guided you
to the most
beautiful places
and people?

remember how things
seemed to unfold
in ways you
never dreamed?

hardships can lead
to hidden pockets
of goodness.

you are always
on the path.

she made it out of there,
not unscathed.

but with beautiful scars,
otherwise known
as her superpowers.

a. quinn

the old magnolia
with weathered
and complex roots.
offered her a safe space.

and so she sat
beneath its green
leathery leaves
and branches
for some time.

and the tree
held her
and soaked up
all her tears.

and then bloomed
with velvety sweetness.

showing her
how to turn
her grief
into beauty.

grace washes over
and she can finally let go.

breaking and dissolving
into the shoreline.

leaving behind
the debris
she carries.

knowing she'll be pulled
back out
into union
with the living water
and rise
all over again.

she tried,
but she couldn't save
anyone else.

and it took her years
to see it all,
to let all of it go,
to let them go.

realizing,
the only person
she had the power to change
was herself,
so she started there.

those old lands
i left,
they never let me heal.
this spirit within
leads me to the open sea,
to the strong and wild waters
built of waves and rhythms and unknowns.
and i fight or float
depending on the winds,
while learning to trust.
in the One who numbered the stars,
in the One who tells the sun to rise,
in the One who lights my path
with lanterns of faith, hope and love.

i want to be enveloped
by the evening orange glow
with the salt of the ocean
layered on my skin.
and saturated by
the morning dew
of the mountain air,
inhaling the silence
and mystery of the forest.
and savor coffee
from the cottage
in the secret garden
that smells of
old books and lilacs.
with my words
and the weeping willow
that understands this grief.
i want the moments
so bursting
with inconceivable goodness
that i cannot possibly
contain any of it.
not for a second.
and i am reminded
i was made to dream wild.
i was made for beauty.

your story is not over.
for a long while,
it seemed like death
would have its way.
but your story lives.

and it lives with a tenacious, underlying pulse.
asking you to feel what must be felt,
at your own pace,
in your own time,
so that you may move forward.

this first half of life has shaped you
in ways you are still naming.
and because of this,
your body has become a magnificent vessel,
one that holds so much grief and love.

may you honor it all.
the pain, the lessons, the beauty,
and your desire, for not only life,
but for the fullest living imaginable.
you have everything you need
to step into this next part,
gently and with quiet strength,
one step at a time.

light.

light the candle.
one flame for you
and one for me.
make the space.
connect to breath.
notice the fire within
and the earth beneath.
safety is here.
love surrounds.
reclaim and rise.
this, the task.
for this sacred day.

-ritual

know where you came from.
take a risk on something wild,
something you feel in your gut.
get quiet and ask the universe
for discernment.
ask your higher self
for guidance.
trust with each small step
that the path will appear.
and finally,
be open to possibilities
that you never even considered.
head up.
shoulders back.
deep breath.
this is your one life.
may you live it.

sometimes it takes a while,
to catch up
to the miracle
unfolding
before us.

because it doesn't look like
we thought it would.

because grief stays
as long as it needs to.

until we are ready and willing
to ask ourselves
a different question.

instead of,
"why do i have to go through this?"

we begin to ask,
"what goodness and beauty might i
be able to bring forth
because of this?"

it was in the removal
of masks
and the emptying
of herself
out onto the page.

she began to feel
the fullness
of joy
and what it meant
to be truly alive
in her own skin
for the first time.

and everything else
was just everything else.

the truth is,
at first and for a while,
it is lonely and messy
and maybe the bravest thing
you will ever do.

to love yourself
back together.

down the winding river
i flow,
side to side,
bank to bank,
from struggle to acceptance,
over and over again.

i am doing
everything i can
to undo what
you've done,
to do things
differently.
despite the harm
you inflicted,
i can see
your beauty.
i suppose
some of you
will always
live in me
and the fact
that i'm ok
with that
tells me
i'm healing.

when things become too heavy
for my body to carry,
i write.
my left hand knows things
my head has yet to process,
allowing me to turn towards
my own heart
instead of against it.

she could see now,
a new vision
for her life
was unfolding,
one she imagines
and brings forth
with the help of others,
those wanting and willing
to walk with her
and she with them.

a vision which
could only emerge
into its fullness,
when she was ready
to accept
that the old dream
had died.

look at all it has taken
for you to get to this point.
all of the learning, the receiving
the listening, the sharing
the moving, the writing
the praying, the lamenting
the loving, the forgiving
the creating, the grieving

all of the growing
has been in the struggling.

it's ok to feel proud
with how far you've come,
even with so much
more work left to do.
and when you feel like
you're failing or falling,
remember this,
it's ok to be
in "the no longer
but not yet" space.
the middle of your story
is a fine place to be.

what if we spoke
our deepest desires aloud?

what if we could watch our shame
disappear into thin air,
transforming into floating notes
of a new melody?

what if we are all songs,
already written,
just waiting to be sung?

she is not interested
in talking about
the weekend plans
or the weather.

she wants to know
who you are
and where you came from.

she wants to know
how your heart
has been shattered
and how you made it through
to sit at this table
drinking coffee together.

some of us
need to hear
that it is ok
to take up space.

it is ok to be in need.
it is ok to ask for help.
it is ok to share your reality
in safe places.
it is ok to be messy.

because even with all of that,
you are enough.

along the way,
we learn
to play small.

shame seeps in
and stealthily disperses,
leaving us
to make the brutal decision
to abandon ourselves.

because being our truest
brings feelings
that we will do
just about anything
to avoid.

so we hide in conformity
until we can't anymore.
because inauthenticity
becomes intolerable.

a wild mare
never fit in
with the ponies
anyway.

you are the mountain
and the ocean.
you are chaos
and conundrums.
you are the softness of dawn
and the gold light
brushed upon the fields.
you are the peace
and the mystery
of the dark side
of the moon.
you are the strength
of the tree
and the fragility
of the poppies.
you are the resilience
of the sunrise
and the grit of the gravel
on this road you walk.
you are words and silence
and organized stardust,
and enough.

she was a living
breathing poem.
what she held
in her body
was both
tragic and magic.

her learning
how to hold
all that tension
is what made
it all so beautiful.

poetry
is mystery
and surprise
and everywhere.

if you're open to it,
you never know
when the words
could run out of your hands
and onto the paper.

not all healing
needs to be heavy and intense.

sometimes it's remembering
how to play.

she stood on top
of the mountain
with streaming tears
and profound gratitude,
for so much more than
just the easy things
she received as blessings
over the years.

she felt the crisp air
brush her face
as she inhaled
the surrounding glory
of the nearly bare trees,
releasing their leaves,
displaying in plain form
the grace and beauty
of vulnerability and change.

she knew that in time,
just as the trees,
she would blossom again
with rich shades of green
and new life
in deeper ways
than ever before.

when your heart
is broken,
i hope you
let yourself
sit with
the cracked edges.

leave the wounds
exposed and weeping
and watch the light
pour in through
all the spaces.

breathe and feel
all the love.

it's not lost,
it's just a lot to hold.
and you see it now,
how much you loved,
how much love exists,
more clearly now
than ever.

shattered hearts
find relief
by tending
to the divine fire
that still burns
from within.

they are
the artists,
the truth tellers,
and the hope holders.

reclaiming
and reimagining
every ragged piece
of their story
for beauty.

when uncertainties arise,
leaving her without peace,
she walks the edge.

between the land
and the sea
to watch the pelicans glide
and the sun slip
gracefully away.

and soon
she comes back home
to herself
with gratitude
and relief.

as she is reminded
to settle into the sand
that shifts beneath her feet,
guided by the waves,
pulled by the moon,
and beyond her control.

sticks and stones
and stories and skin,
thin skin.
it bruises and wounds with ease.
it collects and swells and stings
and some call it weak.
but its sensitivity
is also what allows,
for depth and feelings
to shift about this body
like a gentle breeze.
a tender nature, giving way,
for light to soak through
and emerge from within.

and while each lesson
builds her a stronger backbone,
she beholds her soft and porous
thin skin
with new found delight.

the mystery
of the natural world
is that it is both
divinely chaotic
and stunningly
strung together
in perfect order.

and if she too
was created
by the same creator,

why would she think
she is any different?

it is a cunning trap
we fall into,
the screaming lie
of limitation.

when everything
just under the surface
whispers to us
the truth
of infinite abundance.

strength is.

in the faithful willingness.
it lives in the steps we take
before we think we are ready to take them.

in the courageous "yes".
it lives in the showing up
and the tending of seeds
we cannot yet see.

in the unrelenting hope.
it lives knowing
that in the darkness
the light will always come.

and in the perseverance.
it lives in the "hell no"
of whatever tries
to get in the way.

it says,
"i will grow anyway."
go back to your roots and remember,
you are a child
of the master gardener.

when our souls
leave this earth
and we get to where
we are going,
promise me,
you'll heal,
so you'll come find me.

but i won't be
on the field
of never enough,
with painted white lines
and panting sideline wolves,
where i never belonged.

you'll find me
in a flower field.

and you'll know it is me
because i am the tall mare
with untamed hair,

the wild white horse
of rescue
i had to learn to be
for myself.

like how you hold that newborn baby,
with awe,
gently and tenderly,
with both hands and full of support.

i hope you hold
all the parts
of your own body
that way,
especially your face.

those soft shadows under your eyes,
where fears and tears carved creases over time,
those areas.
the tangible signs
of a courageous life lived.

they've helped you carry and grieve
the insurmountable.
they've worn out brave
and deserve the name,
Beautiful.

tell me your story.
so i can hear
and bear
the echoes
of my own cries.
and feel your tears
run down
my face.

come walk with me,
over edges of grandeur,
with uphill paths and unexpected detours,
you will find your grit and your eyes again.

where it's soft or rocky,
i will show you the way.
with beats and breaths,
you will find your heart
and your footing.

where the sagebrush grows
like a blanket that hugs this land,
and where the light leaks through the aspens,
you will find your soul invigorated again.

where the vibration of this mountain
meets every sense in your body,
you will know rhythm
and interconnectedness.

let me lead you,
just listen for the water,
it is hidden
and better than you imagine.

-spirit guide

the water flows downstream with ease and purpose,
carrying with it,
the dead and the living,
in the shallow and the deep.

it keeps on keeping on,
while singing with rippling and rushing
sounds that soothe,
not unlike my time here, my life here,
that presses on day by day, year by year,
sometimes dragged and pulled against
by my own resistance,
by my own expectations.

what does this say about the one
who created these waters
that never cease in moving forward?
and how do the faithful ones reply?

and maybe to be human,
is to know when
to lay back,
lift my chin,
stretch out my legs,
and float down the river.

wild hair
and an untamed heart,
she flows
so beautifully
in the opposite direction,
a free spirit.

it is clear
she is still
so strongly tethered
to her creator.

her glory,
reveals His.

and she teaches us
how to simply be
among the wildflowers,
reminding us
of who we are
and to whom
we belong.

no matter where
we are
on the journey,

we are always
following someone
ahead of us,
walking with someone
beside us,
or showing someone else
the way.

may we press on,
knowing there will be
more chapters,
ones we cannot see alone
because we need others
to help us dream them up.

the past was never
going to make perfect sense
to her human mind
and it was not hers
to figure out.

over time,
it became clear
that all along
she was being carried,

to this place,
in this time,
to do these things.

with her heart open,
a sword in one hand,
and a white flag in the other.

to really look at her,
is to see a lifetime
of poems hidden
behind her eyes.
all that she carries,
yet to be spoken.
in lines and spaces.
between years of stories
and rivers of wisdom.
between songs of grief
and gardens of beauty.
her dreams sit somewhere
between the oceans
and the mountains.
she is waiting for you
to ask her
if you can come inside.

she didn't have time to waste.
she wanted to be
with those kinds of people,
the ones who had
gone through something
and come out
on the other side,
different.

the ones
owning and sharing and re-writing
their broken stories.

the ones
holding space
for grief and growth and wonder.

the ones
wearing crowns of beauty
for ashes.

i wander these woods,
unknown.
the evergreens dusted
with delicate white,
whispering the way.
forty steps softened
by pillows of fallen pine
and the creek nearby,
flowing.
my exodus.

what is it i fear
will arise in the silence?
not only on the uninhabited
path i walk,
but in the undiscovered
spaces of my mind.

the wilderness i walk
and the wilderness within,
it is becoming difficult
to tell the difference.

either way,
i am believing
you will meet me there.

our wounds, in time,
can become our greatest
allies and assets.

they teach us things
we would not learn
in their absence.

once we begin to heal,
we see how they can help us
live with a new kind of awareness.

an awareness in regards
to ourselves, to God,
to others,
and the interconnected world
in which we live.

we connect dots,
one by one,
to realize the wholeness of our lives.

and we finally see,
that we are part of something larger,
something already within us,
and that we have always
belonged.

it has taken her
all this time to see,
what has been there all along.

in the depths of darkness,
her body spoke and she listened.
a nudge, here and there,
waves of curiosity.

beneath all the layers,
under the cloaks of fear and illusions of control
that allowed her to withstand for so long,
there she is, a survivor.

releasing now what no longer serves her,
turning towards herself with kindness,
finding the child within,
the one romanced by the glow
of fireflies in the night sky.

where her brokenness and beauty
inevitably intersect.
where her strength and softness meet.

she is simultaneously
remembering and becoming.

you have been down there
long enough,
my dear.

it is time
and it is ok,
to look up
from right
where you are.

the miracle is here.
it is in you.
it is you.

-arise

her suffering
so intertwined
with the path of creation
that the idea of making things
seemed like
the only way out.

her voice could no longer
be silenced
and her wounds needed tending
from the light.

so, she made art,
only the art was making her.

not random, these words,
that spew from my lips,
collected and harvested
over time.

through long days
and dark nights
they made the journey
onto the page.

and i speak them
because i cannot
hold them down.

note by note,
they climb out
of my mouth
shouting,
"here i am."

and through the shadows
and the flickers of
the light between the trees,
it turns out,
i want to live
in the land of the living.

Alysia Quinn is a poet whose writing speaks of healing, grief, trauma, and the path of self-discovery. It is her mission to share her authentic voice and story through creative writing. She hopes that her work offers a source of encouragement, strength, meaning, and beauty to those walking a healing path.

for more, visit www.alysiaquinn.com
@alysiaquinnpoetry